Tips on How to Promote eBooks And Market Effectively

M. Naveed

Mendon Cottage Books

JD-Biz Publishing

Entrepreneur Book Series

Table of Contents

Introduction

Books have been written and read since time immemorial. Reading is considered to be an important part of many people's lives. But with the advent of the internet and information technology the concept of books has evolved and transformed into a new product called the e-book. Available online or in virtual soft copies, the access of such books is much easier and convenient for people of the smart era. Many mediums and websites are available for sharing of reading material over the internet. Kindle is one of the most popular e-book series in the world these days. Amazon.com was the creator and marketer of this famous online wonder. Kindle is a special smart device that allows its users to buy, download, browse through and simply read different e-books. In addition people can also benefit from Kindle and use it as a source for newspaper, magazine, and various other types of blogs. You can also use it to access other media websites and digital networks. The Kindle is a specialized hardware that is available in different models and versions. Some are even based on android operating systems like other smart devices. Kindle books are available at Amazon.com.

What is Amazon

Today amazon has become the most popular and largest shopping mall in the world. There are lots of people who buy goods and place orders everyday on amazon. Amazon makes shopping easier because with just a few mouse clicks you can order any item that you may need and it gets delivered to your doorstep within a few days.

Books, DVD's and electronics are the most common products that sell on amazon. Many people do not understand how amazon makes money. This remains a mystery to many people because such a company requires a lot of funds to maintain and conduct its operations. However it is important to understand that amazon has hundreds of dozens of patents on ecommerce processes and by understanding this many people prefer that the company remains a public domain. It is important that we understand how the company is different from other e commerce websites especially when it comes to making money online. We also need to understand amazon's technology infrastructure and how the infrastructure is able to support its multi prolonged business when it comes to online sales.

Amazon has different platforms where both small and large sellers are able to sell their products. At amazon's marketplace there are sellers who offer their goods at a fixed price while in amazon's auction sellers sell their products to the highest bidder. There is also what is known as amazon shops where used goods are sold at fixed prices. If a product appears in all these sites then the product appears in the box that is beside the amazon.com item so that the buyer is able to see whether there is another seller who is selling the product at a cheaper price. The amazon advantage site allows sellers to sell their new movies, books and music directly from the amazon warehouse instead of selling them from their homes or even stores. A seller of that product must first ship a number of units to amazon so that amazon can handle the sales transaction when buyers make orders for that product. When the sales transactions are complete amazon gets a share of the total sales transaction or about 10 to 15 % percent of the total order but the fees may increase due to subscription fees and listing fees.

What is Kindle?

Kindle being a new trend in the digital industry has a lot of potential for growth and innovation. Users can also utilize the income generation benefits of this book's platform. If you are a writer and have the potential to get your book published in the electronic form using the power of Kindle then you should definitely give it a try. But the question is how to go about it? Writing and drafting the book is only the first part of it. This first part will be similar to normal book writing. The difficult task is to make your writing successful and popular. Promoting it on the Amazon Kindle is the prime factor that will help you make some money.

The market of books hosted by Amazon has a tremendous room for many. If you are good writer this is one opportunity that should not be missed. However it cannot be denied that like all other thriving markets, there is a huge competitive environment in it. You need to make your product or e-book attractive and lucrative for the users to read it. Although you will have to employ the traditional methods of online promotion like search engine optimization there are some specific strategies that you will have to follow to make your eBook a success.

Let us have a look at how to enhance the visibility and demand of your product:

Cover

Like any other book or product the packaging of the book says a lot. Similarly the cover of Kindle book is as important as in an ordinary book. The book cover usually has the title of the book and it is the element that is present on the search results when people browse the Amazon market. It has been proven through studies and researches that book covers that are bright and attractive tend to get more clicks than simple and dull covers. The clicks are also important because people may not actually buy the book but their visit makes it more popular. The more popular the book the better chances of it getting more buyers.

Title

Whenever Kindle users search for books, the title and the cover are the only elements of the books that appear on the list. Thus this is the first impression or outlook of the book. Like any other online website, search engine optimization here plays a key role. Your book title should contain the appropriate keywords for it to appear on higher ranks of the search list. This does not mean the keyword stuffing is required. Use words wisely and intelligently. It should make sense to catch the attention of the user. It should be attractive for the user. There should be an effective human factor in it as the users are not bots but people who are using their brain to select a book. So title should grab their attention and provoke their curiosity and urge them to see the details of the book. Like book covers, book titles will also contribute towards more clicks and visitors leading to better sales and success.

Description

Once the cover and title of the book has attracted the user successfully, the next thing that they will access is the description of the book. You need to draft your e-book description keeping in mind the keyword density but not stuffing it with key words. It should be written carefully highlighting the main points of the book in a concise and understandable manner.

Tags and Reviews

Tags and reviews are very important elements present on the product preview page of the Amazon market. Tags can also be keyword oriented but there are considerations that should also be kept in mind. Before devising the tags you should analyze what a potential reader would be searching for in your book. Use these as keywords and phrases. Reviews are very important to convince the potential buyer that your book is good. You can obtain reviews by giving out free samples of your book to people in exchange for a commitment to write good reviews. Good reviews lead to higher ratings and better chances of sales.

Keywords for Optimization

Like any other online website or page keywords play a vital role in the Amazon book market as also use the improvement methods provided by Amazon.com. For example you can carry out a related search and check the appropriateness of your selection of keywords.

You should ensure that there is a perfect match of the keywords with your e-book.

The KDP Select

KDP select is a special service offered if you are making your e-book exclusively for Kindle. This is a great source of free promotion and publicity. It assists in reaching out to a wider audience and potential customer base. Although you are not selling the book directly there are other allied benefits of this process.

It will allow you to list your book for free for 5 days within a 90-day period. This will help you gain more reviews and publicity and increase the popularity. The service lets you lend out your e-book to premium customers of amazon. If Amazon Prime members like your book they are sure to buy it again and also spread a good word around.

Listmania

Creating a list and adding your book to it can get you some good promotion. You can also ask your family and friends to help you in this regard. When more people add it to their lists its popularity is sure to rise. Listmania might have many book lovers who might click on it and ultimately end up buying it for themselves.

Amazon facilitates authors by providing a blogging service for them. You can write an effective blog about your book and gain recognition and publicity. Becoming a popular and liked author compels potential readers to buy your book.

Discussion Forums

By engaging in discussions with potential buyers you are in a better position to convince them to buy your book.

Social Media Marketing

In this era of information and technology social networking is an unavoidable phenomenon. It is also a great way to promote your products and services. Similarly social networks like Facebook and Twitter and other such forums can be used to bring traffic to Amazon listings and publicize your book.

Offering Giveaways

Planning and execution of a giveaway plan can help you yield the required publicity and promotion for the success of your book. For this to materialize you must first use social media to publicize your book and gain the recognition that is required. Giveaways are very fruitful promotional tactics that have been trialed and tested by many successful authors in the past. This process helps improve the potential buyers and readers of the e-book through Facebook likes, followings on Twitter, friends and networks, pinterest followings, subscription on blogs and much more. Anyone who shows a little interest can be treated as a potential buyer and targeted for direct marketing.

1. The first and foremost thing is to have your own or the book's blog. You can create this using blogger, WordPress or any other service provider. The next step is to register with feedburner and add your blog's URL address. Next you need to press the publicize button and the subscription of email. First you should carryout the activation and then check the preview. A pop up of the address will appear which you should save separately. This is the link that will keep people updated about your blog notifications.

2. The second step is to get your own (author) user account on Facebook where you can make various posts about the book and its contents. Save the URL address.

3. You can also create an author's page on Facebook and get users to like it. Save its URL address.

4. Next you need to carry out a creation process of author's accounts on other social networks like Twitter and pinterest. Save the URLs and share information about your book in the accounts.

5. On Facebook you can create an event for the launching ceremony of the book as well. One good suggestion would be to give free copies of the book with some promotional card for Amazon.com. This kind of promotional campaign will attract more people to your giveaway. It does not have to be very expensive. Keep it in accordance with your budget. Once you have decided on this you need to plan the options for entry into the giveaway. The entry options for the giveaway can be the social media accounts created earlier. In today's era of

internet and social networking every individual is attached with one social medium of another. So by adding links that you saved earlier you can facilitate the people to enter the giveaway. The larger the number of entry options the greater the probability of a larger number of people signing up.

6. The next step is post the giveaway details on your created blog. You should use your blog URL and present three additional entry options with it. One is on Pinterest, one on Twitter and one for Facebook. You can now make contacts with other bloggers with similar themes and post advertisements of your book and giveaways of various websites.

7. Another very effective medium for publicizing your book is the Goodreads giveaway. This is an easy process. All you need to do is log on to the book page of Goodreads and enter the "list a giveaway list" option. The giveaway should be carefully planned and should end right before the actual book release. Goodreads has the mechanism to inform all members about the release date of a particular book automatically.

Making Money Using Amazon Kindle E-Book

The Fiction Category

At a Glance:

a. Series of at least 5 books

b. Each book should have at least 20000 words

c. You can write yourself or hire other authors to do so

d. You need to include cliffhangers in your writings

e. You should keep releasing the books at a minimum two week interval and price them at $0.99

f. Make sure reviews are regular and before the release of the next part

g. Every part of the book should have previous and next story links to books

h. You can provide email signing up option to the readers and offer promotional products for new sign ups like new books at lesser costs.

i. The first book should be totally free of cost and the subsequent parts should rise in price gradually. For example first part is free, second is greater than $0.99, third, fourth and fifth parts should be greater than $2.99.

The Length of the Book

On average each book should have 20,000 to 30,000 words. This is an optimal length which will not increase the cost of hiring a freelancer, nor would it take a long time to be written. Short books are very popular and are present in all subjects and fields. As mentioned earlier the duration between the release of two subsequent parts should not be more than two weeks. Hence keeping the book short will help you meet this deadline easily. Any additional words might create difficulty in accomplishment and any decrease in word count can lead to negative reviews noting that the book is too short.

The Genre of the Book

There are a variety of subjects and topics that you can base your book on. It could be mystery, romance, thriller, suspense, horror and many others. The story should be interesting and the series should make the users continue reading in different parts. The cliffhanger is essential at the ending of each book to leave the reader wondering. It will create curiosity, which will lead him to buy the next part. Mystery and thriller are two of the most liked genres in the fiction category. You can write many stories on them and link them to make a series.

The Title of the Book

The book should be titled in accordance to the series requirements. The two parts of the title will include the name of the book and the name of the series.

The Book Cover

Because it is a book series, the book covers of the different parts should be similar. This will promote recognition of the entire series on its own. By looking at the cover of one part readers will be able to tell which series it belongs to. The book cover should also be in accordance with the category of the book list available on Amazon.com. Make sure you select a writing font that is suitable for your genre and is licensed to be used publicly.

Book Content

The layout and design of the inside of the book is pretty important as well. The start of the book should have your email link and the URLs of all other books in this series. Similar information should be present at the end of the book as well. This is very important to improve sales and potential customer growth. You can also provide promotional ads in the start. Once the book becomes permanently free of cost you will receive a great number of email sign up requests.

You can follow the setup format in this way to make it effective:

{Title of the book}

{Name of author}

{Copyright}

Only $0.99 for my new releases

Book 2

Book 3

Book 4

{Content of the Book}

Only $0.99 for my new releases

Book 2

Book 3

Book 4

Outsourcing or Writing the Book

The book can be written by the author himself or he can outsource it to freelancers. There are many websites where you can find good quality affordable writers.

Pricing the Book

Many people suggest not putting the book on KDP select. You can price the book according to a series. This means the first book can be free of cost and the next one can be priced at $0.99 and there can be a gradual increase from there on. This is only done once the entire five book series is complete. But if the books are releasing for the first time then you can charge a nominal amount for every book. You can only apply the gradual pricing strategy once at least three books of the series have been launched.

Book Reviews

Reviews about the book are essential for the success of the book. It puts the book on a smooth selling path. Good reviews are key to increased sales. A good ranking would be near 3.5 or 5 stars. One strategy that you can implement is to search for similar books on the Goodreads and check for critics or people who have awarded them (5) fives. You can contact them and ask them to review your book. You can offer the review writer a free copy of the book in return for a good review from his side. This process should be done before the actual release of the first book. This will ensure that once the book comes out reviews will be ready to be presented to potential buyers. If the reviews are good and the readers liked the story then keep them lined up for the next books in the series. Such persons will leave the review and get the copy for the next book.

Strategy for Release of the Book

One of the most important events of the process is the release of the book. The book release of the series of five books should be done with two weeks in between each book. In this way there will be two books released in 30 days. The promotion and advertising done by Amazon increases when the book is released within a 30-day period.

These are some of the best methods and guidelines that can help promote your fiction e-book on the Amazon network. This is how you will attract potential clients and grow sales.

Kindle: the Non-Fiction Category

Non-fiction is a much more difficult category of book writing. It is not a very good selling product. It takes more effort to attract potential buyers to it. But if you have made the decision to write a non-fiction book it is advisable not to put it on the KDP select.

The Series

The aim should be to select a series of books on similar topics that relate to the same category or subject. This will ensure that if a person buys one book he might also be interested in buying the other books in the series as well. The creation of series in the non-fiction category is much easier as there is no restriction for word. The average word count ranges from 6,000 to 10,000 words.

The various titles for a series of non-fiction books could be as follows:

Main theme or topic is Losing Weight

- *Weight loss techniques for red meat lovers*
- *Weight loss techniques for white meat lovers*

- *Weight loss techniques for vegetable lovers*
- *Weight loss techniques for exercise lovers*
- *Weight loss techniques for pasta lovers*

The Book Content

The best strategy that is currently prevalent in the e-book industry is selecting a topic or subject and then finding information about it on the internet. This will help you create a book of your own. The key here is that to avoid any violation of copyrights laws you should not just copy and paste. Make it simple and analyze the collected information and write it down in your own words.

The set up format of the book should be like the following:

{Title of the Book}

{Name of the Author}

{The Copyright}

The new releases from same author at only $0.99 {Names and links}

{Content of the Book}

The new releases from same author at only $0.99 {Names and links}

Once you have made the selection for the title or subject of your book, you should then start working on the first book of the series. The first book should always be an overview of the selected title. It should also contain information about the later series but should not get into too many details. Just give an overall view. In every subsequent part you can work out the details of the subject in discussion. Thus if you consider the example that we used in the title section, the first book will be about general weight loss. It will have a page or paragraph about weight loss techniques for pasta lovers or vegetarians but not any details. The detailed information will be shared in the later books of the series.

Pricing Strategies

Like fiction, you can offer your first book free of cost, but the for the second book of the series you can charge a nominal amount like $0.99 and all further additions should be priced at $2.99.

Book Cover

As already mentioned in the fiction section in details, the importance of book covers in the selling proposition stage cannot be ruled out. They make the first impression on the potential readers and buyers. This is how people have judged books for so many years. According to the surveys carried out on various platforms including Amazon, more than 70% of all book readers and buyers select a book based on its outer cover. Thus the importance of the book cover has been established. Now the question is how do you design your cover? The answer is it is pretty easy. You should have a look at some of the most successful non-fiction books offered by Amazon and have an analytic look at their covers. This will provide you an idea on how to go about designing your own book series covers.

Book release

This is one of the most vital processes of the book completion and promotion. Same as the case with fiction, you need to release the books in the series with a two-week gap. This will keep your books in the 30-day bracket and you will get lots of free publicity with Amazon.com.

Book Reviews

The process procuring reviews of non-fiction books is different from fiction. One strategy is to use your Facebook account. Give reviews to other book writers in return for your own book review. All you need to do search for book review pages and accounts on Facebook and post your book to join the Facebook group.

After the above discussion it is quite clear that writing a nonfiction book is pretty simple if you follow a simple guideline and process. The key to making money by using Amazon or Kindle is to come up with the books with very short intervals and hence get maximum marketing from amazon. Create one book first and then link the rest of the series with it.

Getting Reviews for your Book

As we have discussed, earlier books reviewed by readers and critics play a very important role in their market success and sales. So providing potential buyers with good reviews about the book you are trying to sell increases your marketing chances. But getting reviews can be a difficult task. Below are some easy and convenient ways to get book reviews:

Back Matter

At the end of your book, you can ask readers to provide a review. This is possible both on Kindle and Nook. All you have to do is add a review request on the last page of your book.

Linkedin

Linkedin is a popular social network site that provides a platform for receiving and giving book reviews. You can go to http://www.linkedin.com/groups/Book- Reviewers-1521067 and find what you are looking for.it

Facebook Groups

Another great place to get some good book reviews for your book is Facebook group https://www.facebook.com/groups/reviewseekers/.

Arrange a Giveaway

We have already mentioned in detail how you should plan a giveaway and use it to promote your book. You can also carry out a giveaway on a website, sit back and get some reviews from the readers.

Search for Top Rated Amazon Reviewers

Amazon is a large platform where you can search for book reviewers who have reviewed books similar to yours. Submit your books to them and ask for some reviews. For every five books you have the chance to get at least one or two return reviews. The list is available at http://www.amazon.com/review/top- reviewers.

Find your Own Reviewer:

Look around your community, family members, friends, friends of friends, coworkers or even complete strangers and search for book readers and ask them to review your book. Indicate that there is no obligation or compulsion; it is a simple request made on a social basis. You do not need a very technical review from them. It can be a simple understanding and liking for the written material. As a member of Goodreads, you can also get a cross posting option from them too.

Discussion forums:

You can become part of many discussion forums available online and distribute free copies in return for a review. You can reach out through the Goodreads groups, Mobile Reads forums, Nook Boards and Kindle Boards.

Conclusion:

So for all newcomers or new writers that have just started their careers online, e-book writing is similar to writing a traditional book. But the avenues of selling this product are different. Using platforms like Goodreads and Kindle you can launch your books and get a reasonable payback for your efforts. But the process of promotion should be done keeping certain important guidelines in mind. The process of writing the book is simple but the task of promoting it to attract more buyers is still very tricky. So the next time you write an e-book and offer it to readers online, follow the tips provided in the above discussion and work hard for the success of your series.

Our books are available at
1. Amazon.com
2. Barnes and Noble
3. Itunes
4. Kobo
5. Smashwords
6. Google Play Books

Check out some of the other JD-Biz Publishing books
Gardening Series on Amazon

Health Learning Series

Health Learning Series

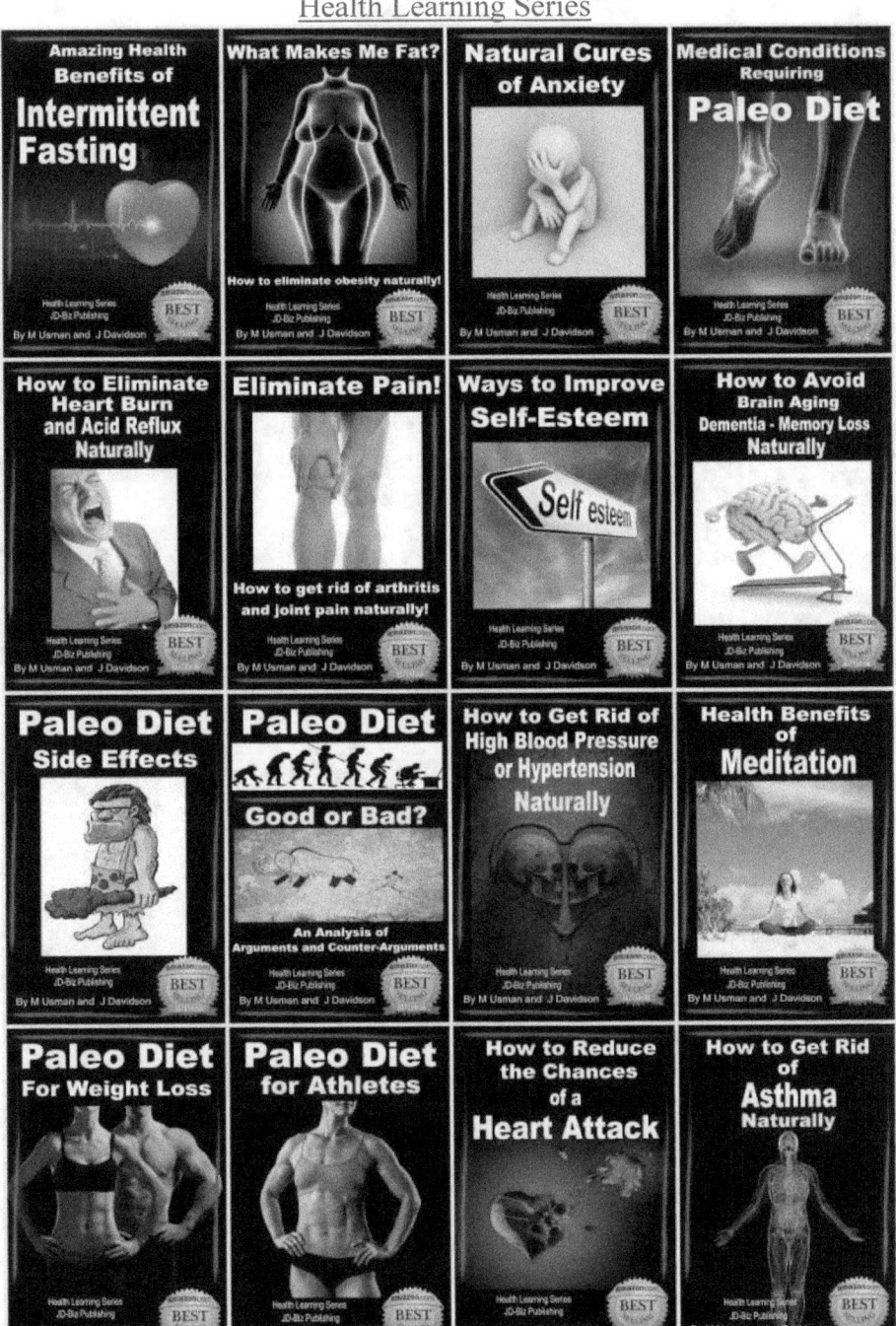

Amazing Animal Book Series

Learn To Draw Series

How to Build and Plan Books

Entrepreneur Book Series

Publisher

JD-Biz Corp

P O Box 374

Mendon, Utah 84325

http://www.jd-biz.com/